Kids Can Do It!

I CAN GROW A GARDEN!

by Ruth Owen

WINDMILL BOOKS

Published in 2018 by **Windmill Books**, an Imprint of Rosen Publishing
29 East 21st Street, New York, NY 10010

Produced for Rosen by Ruby Tuesday Books Ltd
Designer: Emma Randall

Photo Credits: Courtesy of Ruby Tuesday Books and Shutterstock. Cover courtesy of Alamy.

Cataloging-in-Publication Data
Names: Owen, Ruth.
Title: I can grow a garden! / Ruth Owen.
Description: New York : Windmill Books, 2018. | Series: Kids can do it! | Includes index.
Identifiers: ISBN 9781499483512 (pbk.) | ISBN 9781499483451 (library bound) |
ISBN 9781499483345 (6 pack)
Subjects: LCSH: Gardening--Juvenile literature.
Classification: LCC SB457.094 2018 | DDC 635-dc23

Manufactured in the United States of America
CPSIA Compliance Information: Batch BS17WM: For Further Information contact Rosen Publishing, New York, New York at 1-800-237-9932

WARNING:

Some of the activities in this book require adult help. It's also important that all laws and regulations are followed when carrying out the activities in this book. The author and publisher disclaim any liability in connection with the use of the information in this book.

CONTENTS

TIME TO GET GROWING!

If you've never tried gardening or growing a plant, now is the time to get started. You may only have a tiny patch of ground outside your home, a balcony, or even just a doorstep. But if space is limited, that's no problem to a creative gardener.

A garden can be as big as a football field or as small as a single plant pot. What matters is that you're growing and caring for plants, and that's good for you and the **environment**.

Gardening is a great way to be physically active, get some fresh air, and get up close with nature.

From a giant oak tree to a tomato plant, all plants produce the oxygen we need to breathe.

Plants provide food and shelter for wild animals, especially insects.

Plants remove carbon dioxide and other polluting gases from the air.

A QUICK GUIDE TO GARDENING

Gardening may seem a bit mysterious if you've never done it before, but don't be nervous. Growing plants is all about learning and having fun! Here are some important basics to get you started.

What does a plant need to grow?

- A plant needs sunlight.
- A plant needs soil to grow in.
- A plant needs **nutrients**, which it takes in from the soil through its roots.
- A plant needs water.

Potting soil

What equipment do I need to be a gardener?

- Bags of potting soil can be bought from garden centers and other stores. It is used for growing seeds and plants in containers.
- A small spade for digging.
- A pair of tough scissors for any cutting jobs.
- Small flowerpots or recycled containers, such as yogurt cartons, for growing seeds.

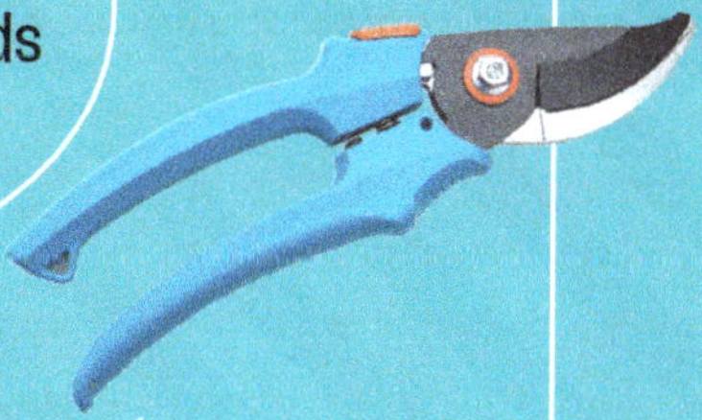

JUNK GARDENING

Plant pots and containers can be expensive to buy. With a little creativity, however, you can turn unwanted junk into some fun and funky planters.

Items such as aluminum cans, chipped coffee mugs, old pans and cooking pots, and even old boots can easily be repurposed.

These types of containers can be used to grow small plants called succulents. They are also perfect for bulbs and annual plants that only grow and flower for a few months.

There are three very good reasons to use recycled containers:

Recycling old junk is great for the environment.

Using junk in your garden saves money for you to spend on seeds and plants.

Gardening with junk gives you a chance to get creative and will make visitors to your garden smile!

Old aluminum can and teacup

Succulent plants

Annual plants

SPRING FLOWER RUBBER BOOTS

Spring bulbs, such as daffodils and tulips, must be planted in the fall. In a very cold area, containers of bulbs can be left in a tool shed or garage until the weather warms up in early spring. In warmer areas, the containers can be left outdoors over the winter.

You will need:

- Old rubber boots
- An ice pick (to be used by an adult)
- A small spade
- Gravel or pebbles
- Potting soil
- Ten miniature daffodil bulbs

1 Ask an adult to help you make six holes in the bottom of each rubber boot. The holes will allow rainwater to escape from the boots so the soil and bulbs do not get too wet.

holes to make water escape

2 Completely fill the toes of the boots with gravel. Also, place a layer of gravel about 1 inch (3 cm) deep across the heel section of the boots.

3 Add about 2 inches (5 cm) of potting soil on top of the gravel. The soil should reach ankle level inside the boots.

4 Place five daffodil bulbs on top of the soil inside each boot.

5 Fill each boot with potting soil up to about 1 inch (3 cm) below the rims.

6 Place a thin layer of gravel over the soil.

7 In spring, place the boots outdoors. Once you see daffodil shoots appear from under the soil, keep the soil moist by watering the containers.

SPRING IS HERE!

In the fall you can buy daffodil bulbs from garden centers, supermarkets, and many other stores. You can also buy them online.

In spring, garden centers and other stores sell lots of small plants, such as pansies and primroses.

Rubber boots planted with spring bulbs

Primrose

Pansy

These plants flower for just a few months. You can fill old boots or shoes with potting soil and plant some of these colorful little plants.

Once the plants stop producing flowers, remove them from their containers. Plant them in soil in a flowerbed and they will flower again next year.

Make sure you ask permission before recycling someone's old shoes or boots as plant containers!

GROW YOUR OWN FRUITS AND VEGETABLES

Growing vegetables is easier than you think. But why grown your own?

Homegrown produce is super fresh because you can eat it within hours of harvesting it. Vegetables you buy in a big supermarket may have been stored for weeks in a warehouse. They may have also been on display for several days in the store.

Fresh homegrown carrots

Store-bought vegetables are often wrapped in plastic or cardboard. When you grow your own, there's no packaging to throw away. Also, homegrown produce cuts down on food waste because you only pick what you need.

Wasteful plastic packaging

A zero food miles salad

Save Food Miles

Food miles are a way to measure how far your food has traveled from where it was grown to your local store. It may have traveled hundreds or thousands of miles (km) on planes, boats, and trucks. All those food miles mean more pollution. Homegrown fruits and veggies produce zero food miles, so they are great for the environment!

GET READY FOR PLANTING

If you're growing vegetables outdoors, you will need to prepare the ground. Dig down to a depth of about 6 inches (15 cm). Keep digging and turning over the soil until it is soft and crumbly. This will help the roots of small **seedlings** spread out to find water and nutrients.

Weeds are tough plants that grow and spread quickly. If you let weeds grow around your plants, they will suck up water and nutrients that your plants need to grow. The weeds may also block out sunlight.

Remove any weeds, tufts of grass, chunks of rock, or pieces of trash.

If you're growing vegetables in a container, make sure the container has holes in the bottom. This will allow excess water to drain through so the soil doesn't get too wet.

Fill the container with potting soil.

Large flowerpots, plastic buckets, wooden boxes, and old baskets or cooking pots can all be used as containers for growing plants.

HOW TO PLANT SEEDS IN POTS

1. Take a small flowerpot, yogurt carton, or other clean, recycled container. If you're using a recycled container, ask an adult to pierce holes in the bottom for drainage.

Used coffee cup

Yogurt cartons

Plastic flowerpot

2. Fill the container with potting soil up to about half an inch (1 cm) from the rim.

3. Place the seeds on the soil. Check the packet to see how many seeds can grow in one pot.

4. Cover the seeds with a thin layer of soil.

The plastic bag creates a mini greenhouse that will keep your pot warm. Condensation will also form on the plastic and drip onto the soil to keep it moist.

5. Place a clear plastic bag over the pot and hold it in place with a rubber band. Set the pot on a dish or tray to catch any water.

6 Label your pot of seeds so you know what they are. Set the pot on a sunny windowsill.

Plastic bag

7 Once the seeds **germinate** and tiny seedlings sprout from the soil, remove the plastic bags.

Seedling

8 Keep checking the pots each day and water them to keep the soil moist.

Read the instructions on the following pages to learn what to do next!

IT'S ALL ABOUT TEAMWORK

Most vegetable seeds are planted in spring or early summer. Because weather and temperatures vary across the country, the dates to plant seeds vary, too. You can check when to plant online or on seed packets. You can also ask for advice at a garden center, or get help from an experienced gardener.

HOW TO GROW TOMATOES

1 Follow the seed planting instructions on pages 12-13. Plant about six tomato seeds in each small pot or container.

Tomato seeds

2 As the seedlings grow, pull out any small or weak plants to leave the biggest, strongest plants.

Tomato seedling

3 Once the plants are about 7 inches (18 cm) tall, plant them in a container of potting soil. Put the plants outside in a warm, sunny place.

A container the size of a bucket will be just right for two tomato plants.

4 Tomato plants need lots of water, so keep the soil moist.

5 Tomato plants grow tall and their stems are bendy. Push some tall sticks, or even an old broom handle, into the soil. As the plants grow, loosely tie their stems to the sticks with string so they are supported.

Did you know tomatoes are actually fruits?

6 Every two weeks, give your plants a boost of nutrients by feeding them some liquid **fertilizer**. You can buy this from a garden center or large supermarket that sells gardening equipment. Follow the instructions on the box or bottle.

IT'S ALL ABOUT TEAMWORK

When using plant fertilizer, ask an adult to help you choose which type to buy. Make sure an adult is close by when you're using the product and ask them to help you find a safe place to store the container.

7 The tomato plants will grow yellow flowers. Then behind each flower, a tomato will start to form.

8 Keep watering and feeding your plants and you'll soon have juicy, red tomatoes ready for harvesting.

If you don't want to grow your own seeds, you can buy small plants that are ready for planting outside. Then you can buy just two or three plants.

GROW FRESH PEAS

1. Begin by planting five pea plant seeds in each small pot or container.

2. Prepare a patch of ground for planting. Push long, sturdy twigs or **bamboo canes** into the ground to form a tepee shape. Wind string around the twigs or canes to make a framework.

3. Once the pea plants are about 7 inches (18 cm) tall, plant two or three at the bottom of each twig or cane.

Pea plants will grow upward around a tepee. They cling to twigs and string with their thin, curly tendrils.

4. Check the plants each day and water the soil to keep it moist.

5. Once the plants have flowered, you will see seedpods forming. You can eat the pods or wait until the peas inside grow fat and juicy.

GROW JUICY SALAD LEAVES

If you're a beginner gardener, the best kind of lettuce to grow is the type you can cut and regrow. Choose a packet of seeds that contains a mixture of different types and colors of leaves.

Lettuce seedlings

1. Fill large containers with potting soil. You can plant lettuce seeds directly where they will grow.

2. Sprinkle lettuce seeds on top of the soil. Then cover the seeds with a thin layer of soil.

Lettuce leaves growing in a container

3. Place the containers in a sunny place and keep them watered.

GROW ZUCCHINI AND PUMPKINS

Zucchini and pumpkins belong to the same plant family. We think of them as vegetables, but like tomatoes, they are actually fruits because they contain seeds.

1. To grow zucchini and pumpkins, begin by following the instructions on pages 12-13. Plant two seeds into each small pot or container.

Zucchini seed

Zucchini plant

2. Once each small plant has three or four leaves, it is ready to be planted in a container or in the ground.

3. A container the size of a bucket is just the right size for one zucchini plant.

4. Put the container in a sunny spot and give it lots of water.

5. The plants will grow big leaves and bright, yellow flowers. Check the flowers and you will see zucchini forming behind some of them.

You can grow green or yellow zucchini. Just check the seed packs.

MAKE A PUMPKIN PATCH

1 Prepare a patch of ground outdoors. Check on the seed pack to learn how much space to allow for each pumpkin plant.

2 Dig a small hole. Remove the plant and its soil from the small pot and place it in the hole. Fill any space in the hole with soil, pat down the ground around the plant, and water.

3 Remove any weeds that grow around your plants and give them lots and lots of water.

4 By October, you'll have your own homegrown pumpkins to carve for Halloween!

CARROTS AND GREEN ONIONS

Carrot and green onion seeds can be directly planted into the ground outdoors.

1. Begin by preparing an area of ground that's about 4 feet by 4 feet (1 m × 1 m).

2. Using a small spade or stick, scrape six narrow trenches, or rows, in the ground from one side of the vegetable patch to the other. The rows should be equally spaced and about 1 inch (3 cm) deep.

Trench, or row, for planting seeds

3. Sprinkle a pack of carrot seeds into three of the rows. Try to space out the seeds as much as possible, but this can be tricky as seeds are very tiny!

4. Sow a pack of green onions into the other three rows.

5. Very gently fill in the rows with loose soil. Water the vegetable patch well.

6 Keep watering the soil to keep it moist, and pull out any weeds between the rows.

7 You will soon have six rows of tiny seedlings. Once the little plants are about 3 inches (8 cm) tall, thin them out. This means pulling out the smallest and weakest plants to give the strongest plants a better chance of growing.

These carrot seedlings are ready to be thinned out.

Keep the vegetable patch free from weeds.

Row of green onions

These carrot seedlings have been thinned out.

8 Keep thinning out the plants as they grow. You should eventually have about 2 inches (5 cm) between each plant.

9 When the onions and carrots have grown, harvest them by gently pulling them from the soil. Only harvest what you want to eat, and try not to disturb the plants on either side.

GROW YOUR OWN STRAWBERRIES

When summer comes, wouldn't it be great to have your own crop of juicy, red strawberries?

You can buy small strawberry plants from a garden center for just a few dollars.

1. Prepare a small patch of ground. An area of about 2 feet by 2 feet (61 × 61 cm) will be suitable for four plants.

A strawberry plant, or root

2. Plant your strawberries in spring and keep them well watered.

Strawberry flowers

3. In summer, the plants will produce small white flowers. You will see fruits forming as the flowers die off.

Straw

New fruits forming

This fruit is ready to pick.

You can place straw around your plants. This keeps the fruits from touching wet ground and starting to rot. The kind of straw you buy for pet bedding is fine for this purpose.

4 Pick the fruits when they are fat and red.

5 The strawberry plants will send out shoots called runners. At the end of each runner are small leaves and roots.

Make small U-shaped pieces of wire.

Press the pieces of wire over the runners.

6 Use a hairpin or U-shaped piece of wire to pin each runner to the ground.

7 The roots on the tiny new plant at the end of the runner will grow down into the soil. Once the new plant has taken root, cut off the runner's stem close to the "mother" plant and the new plant.

Each tiny new plant will be ready to produce strawberries next summer. New plants for free!

CUTE, COLORFUL SUCCULENTS

Succulents are small plants that grow in hot, dry environments, such as deserts and grasslands. They can store water in their fat, fleshy leaves.

You can buy succulents at garden centers and other stores that sell plants.

1. To make a miniature succulents garden, buy or find a bowl or other shallow container. Try looking at thrift stores or yard sales for suitable containers. A bowl with drainage holes in the bottom is best

2. Fill the container up to the rim with a mixture of potting soil and grit. This will create soil that's similar to the plants' natural habitat.

You can buy grit from garden centers, home wares stores, and shops that sell aquarium supplies.

Cover the surface of the soil with more colorful grit.

3. Plant the succulents in the bowl so their leaves are above the rim of the container. This keeps the leaves from getting too wet.

4. Give the plants lots of water at one time, soaking the soil. Then allow the soil to dry out completely before watering again.

In a desert, succulents take in lots of water during a rainstorm and store it in their leaves. They may not get water again for weeks, or longer.

5. You can decorate your miniature garden with shells or beach pebbles. Try painting pebbles with acrylic paints. Add a layer of clear nail polish to seal and protect the design.

GROW A BUTTERFLY GARDEN

Butterflies, bees, and other insects need flowers for food. Create a flower garden that will provide a place to feed for lots of tiny creatures.

Butterflies and other insects visit flowers to drink a sweet juice called **nectar**. As they feed, they help **pollinate** flowers by carrying **pollen** from flower to flower.

Go online to identify the butterflies that live in your area. Then research which plants they like to visit.

GROW A BUTTERFLY GARDEN

Here are some ideas for easy-to-grow, butterfly-friendly flowers.

You can grow your own plants from seeds by following the instructions on pages 12-13.

Buy small plants from a garden center and plant them in your garden.

Some butterfly-friendly plants, such as alliums, grow from bulbs.

Alliums

Cosmos

French marigolds

Lantana

Zinnias

Sunflowers

Buddleia (butterfly bush)

1. Prepare the ground for your butterfly garden by following the instructions on page 11.

2. Research how much space your plants need and how tall they will grow. Check seed packets and plant labels to find out this information.

3. Before you begin planting, draw a plan to follow. Use a small spade or stick to divide up the flowerbed into sections.

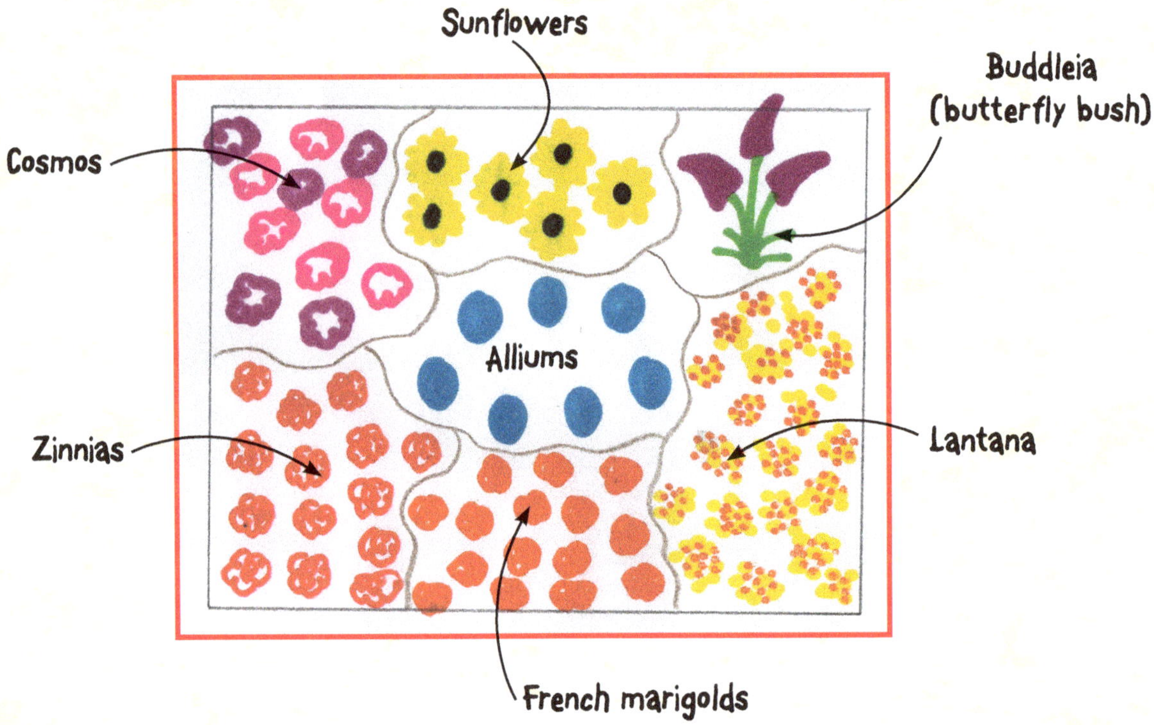

Sunflowers don't only provide nectar and pollen for insects. They also produce seeds that wild birds love to eat.

ENJOY YOUR GARDENING!

Be a neat gardener! Always wash your tools and put them away after working in the garden.

Make sure you wash your hands thoroughly with soap and warm water after gardening.

IT'S ALL ABOUT TEAMWORK

Always ask an adult for permission before you begin work on a garden project. When buying seeds or plants online or at a garden center, always check out your ideas with an adult first.

If a plant dies or your garden plans and ideas don't work out the first time, don't worry. This often happens to experienced gardeners, too.

Just keep trying, learning, and having lots of fun!

GLOSSARY

bamboo canes
Hard, straight, thin stems from bamboo plants that can be used as supports for growing plants. Bamboo canes can be bought from garden centers.

environment
The natural world around us, including the land, air, rivers, lakes, and oceans.

fertilizer
A chemical or natural substance that's added to soil to give plants the nutrients they need to grow.

germinate
Begin to grow. Seeds sprout tiny shoots as they germinate.

nectar
A sweet liquid made by flowers in order to attract insects and other small animals that help with pollination.

nutrients
Substances that a living thing needs to help it live and grow. Nitrogen and potassium are nutrients needed by plants.

pollen
A dust produced by flowers that is needed for fertilization and the production of seeds.

pollinate
To move pollen from the anthers of one flower to the stigma of another flower of the same species. This enables fertilization to take place and seeds to form.

seedlings
Tiny, new plants.

weeds
Plants that are growing where they are not wanted. Weeds are often tough, wild plants that grow and reproduce very quickly.

WEBSITES

For web resources related to the subject of this book, go to:
www.windmillbooks.com/weblinks and select this book's title.